Inside the Brain

Rufus Bellamy

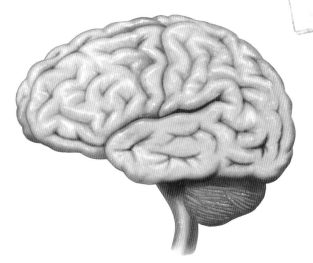

W

FRANKLIN WATTS

This edition 2007

Franklin Watts
338 Euston Road, London NW1 3BH

Franklin Watts Australia
Level 17/207 Kent Street
Sydney, NSW 2000

Copyright © Franklin Watts 2004

Series editor: Adrian Cole
Series design: White Design
Art director: Jonathan Hair
Picture research: Diana Morris
Educational consultant: Peter Riley
Medical consultant: Dr Gabrielle Murphy

A CIP catalogue record for this book is available from the British Library.

ISBN–13: 978 0 7496 7261 4

Printed in Malaysia

Acknowledgements:
Bettmann/Corbis: 15bl. Dee Breger/SPL: 26t. BSIP, Keene/SPL: 16b. Chris
Clarke/Newsflash/Pressnet/Topham: 11b. CNRI/SPL: 12b. Bob Daemmrich/
The Image Works/Topham: 7b, 26b, 27b. Klaus Guldbrandsen/SPL: 7t. Ted
Horowitz/Corbis: 28t. Jacksonville Courier/The Image Works/Topham: 8t. Gabe
Palmer/Corbis: 5t. Alfred Pasieka/SPL: 4t. Philippe Plailly/SPL: 25b. SPL: 10t.
Geoff Tompkinson/SPL: 20t. UPPA Ltd/Topham: 20b. Alesandro
Vinnini/Corbis Sygma: 5b. Wellcome Dept of Cognative Neurology/SPL:
15br. Bo Zaunders/Corbis: 23t. Zephyr/SPL: 13b.
Every attempt has been made to clear copyright. Should there be any
inadvertent omission, please apply to the publisher for rectification.

Franklin Watts is a division of
Hachette Children's Books.

Contents

The brain controls **the body**   **4**

The nervous system links the **brain and the body**   **6**

Nerves are the body's **communication system**   **8**

The spinal cord is the body's **communication highway**   **10**

The brain is the body's **control centre**   **12**

The brain receives and **processes information**   **14**

Movement is co-ordinated by **the brain**   **16**

The nervous system controls **body functions**   **18**

We remember things, make decisions and **have opinions**   **20**

The limbic system helps **produce emotions**   **22**

We have different types of **memory**   **24**

The brain is linked to the **endocrine system**   **26**

Endocrine glands produce **hormones**   **28**

Glossary   **30**

Find out more   **31**

Index   **32**

The brain controls
the body

The brain only weighs about 1.4 kilograms, but it controls our movement, keeps the body functioning properly and lets us understand and communicate with the world around us.

Powerful network
The brain is made up of many billions of nerve cells called neurons that link together into a highly complicated network. The brain functions 24 hours a day and is much more powerful than any computer that has ever been made.

Skull bone
protects the brain

Cerebrum
(see page 13)

Spinal link
This scan shows clearly the join between the brain and the spinal cord, which runs from the base of the brain down the back.

Linked to the body
The brain is joined to the spinal cord, which runs down the back. Both are linked to the body through a network of nerves. Information about what is happening inside and outside the body travels to the brain and spinal cord along these nerves. The nerves also carry instructions from the brain and spinal cord to the body.

Many functions
The brain controls a range of functions, from movement to the production of feelings and emotions. Different parts of the brain do specific jobs, but many functions, such as thinking, involve different areas acting together.

Skull cutaway
The brain is made of soft tissue. It is protected by the hard, bony skull.

THE BRAIN IN ACTION

Nerve impulses move continuously around
the network of neurons that make up the
brain. As this happens the brain produces
tiny electrical signals called brain waves.
Brain waves can be detected by a machine
called an electroencephalograph (EEG).
Scientists can look at the different types
of wave and work out what the brain is
doing and whether it is healthy.

Exam pressure

*During an exam, such as the one being sat here, the
brain produces a lot of brain waves as it recalls
information and thinks.*

Chemical links

The nerves are not the only route through which the brain
controls the body. The brain is also linked to the endocrine
system (see pages 26–27). This produces chemicals, called
hormones (see pages 28–29), that influence things such as our
emotions and food digestion. The brain and the endocrine system
work together to make sure that all these things happen properly.

Day-to-day life

*The people here are using their
brains to control almost all
of their activities, including
walking and talking.*

The nervous system links the
brain and the body

Brain
is part of the central nervous system and continually sends out and receives nerve impulses

Spinal cord
is part of the central nervous system

To do its job properly, the brain communicates continually with the rest of the body. It does this through the spinal cord and a network of nerve cells (neurons) that reaches throughout the body. Together, the brain, spinal cord and the body's network of nerves are called the nervous system. This is divided into two main parts: the central nervous system and the peripheral nervous system.

The central nervous system

The central nervous system is made up of the brain and the spinal cord. It receives nerve impulses (see page 9) from the rest of the body. The brain processes these nerve impulses, compares them with memories and, if necessary, sends out new instructions. These travel down nerves to the body's muscles and organs to tell them what to do.

Central nervous system
brain and spinal cord

System diagram
This diagram shows the different connections between the two parts of the nervous system and the direction in which nerve impulses flow.

Peripheral nervous system
motor neurons carry nerve impulses from the spinal cord and brain

Nerves
form the peripheral nervous system and run between the central nervous system and the rest of the body

Peripheral nervous system
sensory neurons carry nerve impulses to the spinal cord and brain

Nervous system
The nervous system is divided into two main parts: the central nervous system and the peripheral nervous system.

Some motor neurons
carry instructions to muscles to make body movements

Some motor neurons
carry instructions to control 'involuntary' functions (see pages 18–19)

The peripheral nervous system

The peripheral nervous system is made up of the nerves that run to and from the central nervous system. The peripheral nervous system carries nerve impulses from sensory neurons all over the body. The peripheral nervous system also carries the instructions the central nervous system sends out to the rest of the body via motor neurons. When these impulses get to the body's muscles and organs, they produce a response.

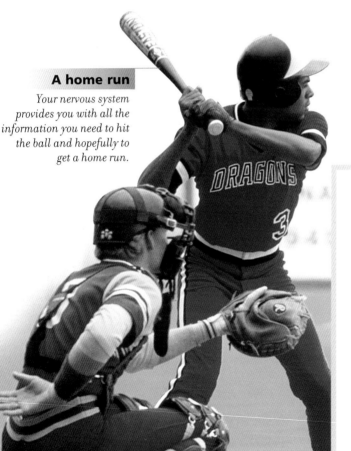

Information carriers

Nerves of the peripheral nervous system, like the ones above, carry nerve impulses all over the body and forge a link between the body and the central nervous system.

A home run

Your nervous system provides you with all the information you need to hit the ball and hopefully to get a home run.

THE NERVOUS SYSTEM IN ACTION

The nervous system allows you to respond to situations. For example, in a game of baseball, your eyes and ears and other sense organs continually send nerve impulses along sensory neurons to your brain. Your brain compares these nerve impulses to its memories of games you have played. It then sends new nerve impulses, at the right time, via the spinal cord and peripheral nervous system to your arm muscles, instructing them to move. When these instructions reach your arms, you swing the bat and hopefully hit a home run.

Nerves are the body's
communication system

Nerves are the 'wires' that link the central nervous system to the rest of the body. There are over 100 kilometres of nerves in the body and they reach all parts of the skin, internal organs and muscles. Nerves can be up to 2 centimetres thick, or thinner than a hair. They are covered in a sheath and contain bundles of nerve cells called neurons.

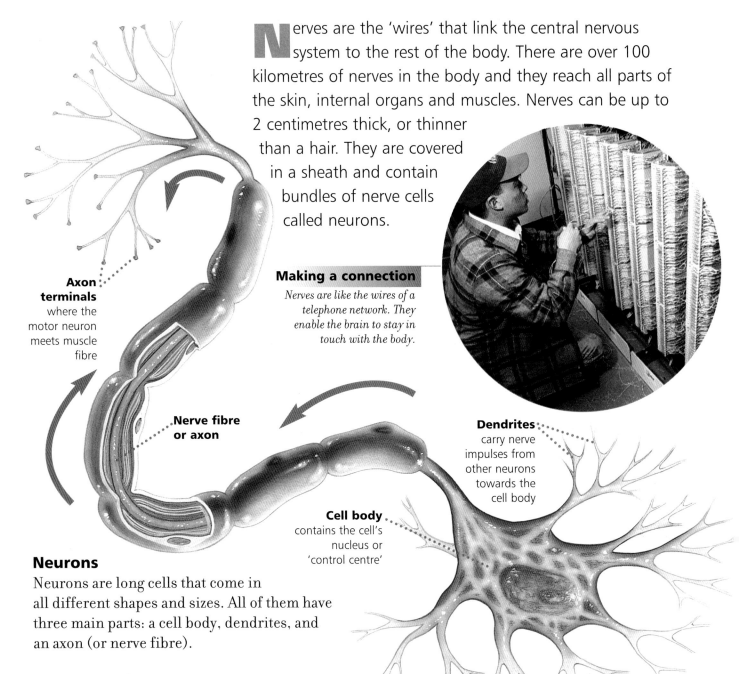

Axon terminals
where the motor neuron meets muscle fibre

Making a connection

Nerves are like the wires of a telephone network. They enable the brain to stay in touch with the body.

Nerve fibre or axon

Dendrites
carry nerve impulses from other neurons towards the cell body

Cell body
contains the cell's nucleus or 'control centre'

Neurons

Neurons are long cells that come in all different shapes and sizes. All of them have three main parts: a cell body, dendrites, and an axon (or nerve fibre).

Sensory and motor neurons

There are two types of neuron in the peripheral nervous system: sensory neurons and motor neurons. Sensory neurons carry information to the central nervous system about what is happening inside and outside the body. Motor neurons carry instructions from the central nervous system to muscles and organs.

A motor neuron

Nerve impulses from the brain and spinal cord only travel in one direction along a motor neuron.

Old cells

Most cells in the body 'die' and are replaced. However, neurons (especially those in the brain and spinal cord) are very different. Most last a lifetime and are not normally replaced if they 'die' as a result of old age, injury or disease. This means that neurons are among the oldest cells in the body and that as we age we have fewer neurons.

Inside a nerve
Nerves, like the one shown here, usually contain both motor and sensory neurons.

Outer sheath
protects the bundles of neurons

Motor neuron
see opposite page

Sensory neuron
carries nerve impulses from the sense receptor to the central nervous system

Blood vessel
supply oxygen and nutrients to the nerve

Sensory receptor
responds to stimuli, such as light or temperature

Muscle fibre

Axon terminals

Motor neuron

Sensory neuron

Direction of nerve impulses

ELECTRICAL SIGNALS

Neurons carry information and instructions in the form of nerve impulses. A nerve impulse is an electrical signal that travels along a neuron (always in the same direction). This happens when a sensory receptor or dendrite at the end of the nerve is stimulated. The brain analyses nerve impulses it receives and sends out new nerve impulses to control the body.

Neurons meet at junctions called synapses, but they do not touch. When a nerve impulse reaches a synapse, chemicals are released. These chemicals cross the gap and start a nerve impulse in the next neuron.

Synapse
is a gap that chemical messages pass across

Nerve impulse in action
Nerve impulses only travel along neurons in one direction. Here, an impulse travels from a sensory receptor to a motor neuron in a reflex action (see page 11).

The spinal cord is the body's
communication highway

The spinal cord is a tube of nervous tissue that runs down the back of the body from the base of the brain to the lower back. It is the main communication highway between the brain and the rest of the body. The spinal cord carries nerve impulses to and from the brain. These impulses enter and leave the spinal cord through nerves, which branch off and run throughout the body. The spinal cord also plays an important role in co-ordinating the body's activity (see opposite page).

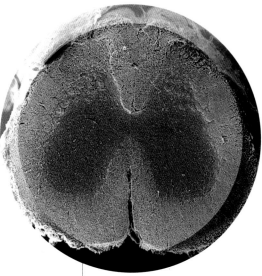

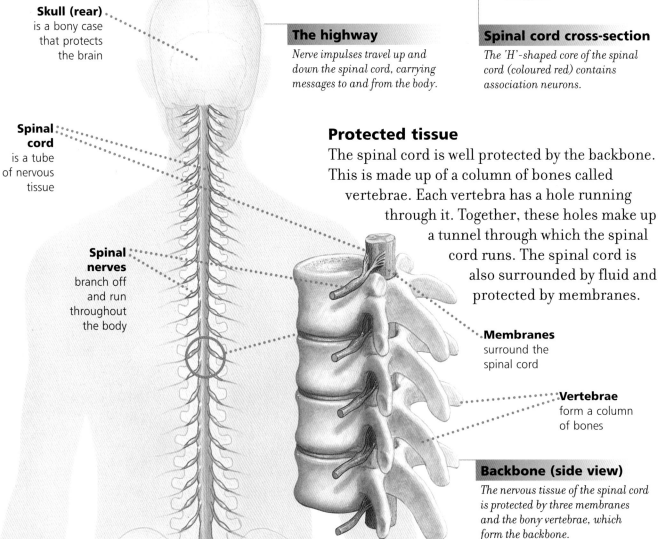

Skull (rear)
is a bony case that protects the brain

The highway
Nerve impulses travel up and down the spinal cord, carrying messages to and from the body.

Spinal cord cross-section
The 'H'-shaped core of the spinal cord (coloured red) contains association neurons.

Spinal cord
is a tube of nervous tissue

Spinal nerves
branch off and run throughout the body

Protected tissue

The spinal cord is well protected by the backbone. This is made up of a column of bones called vertebrae. Each vertebra has a hole running through it. Together, these holes make up a tunnel through which the spinal cord runs. The spinal cord is also surrounded by fluid and protected by membranes.

Membranes
surround the spinal cord

Vertebrae
form a column of bones

Backbone (side view)
The nervous tissue of the spinal cord is protected by three membranes and the bony vertebrae, which form the backbone.

Spinal nerves

Spinal nerves attach to the spinal cord through gaps between each vertebra. These nerves contain sensory and motor neurons. Most sensory neurons enter the back of the spinal cord, while most motor neurons leave at the front.

Spinal cord sections

Inside the spinal cord there are two main areas. The first is an inner, 'H'-shaped core, mainly made up of association neurons (see below). These link the spinal nerves to other nerve fibres. The second area is the outer part of the spinal cord. It is mainly made up of nerve fibres that carry nerve impulses up and down the spinal cord.

Inner layer is 'H'-shaped and contains association neurons

Outer layer is made up of nerve fibres

Spinal nerve

Spinal nerve

Protective membranes

Reflex action

This is how pain causes the spinal cord to 'short circuit', which allows the body to respond quickly.

Spinal cord cutaway

The nervous tissue of the spinal cord forms two clearly defined areas.

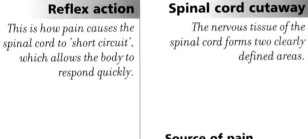

Source of pain

Sensory receptor in the skin

Sensory neuron

Section from the spinal cord

Association neurons transfer impulse to motor neuron

Motor neuron in muscle

REFLEX ACTIONS

Many actions in the body happen automatically without you having to think about them. When you touch something, such as a hot iron or a scary spider, you pull your hand away from it quickly. These 'reflex' actions are co-ordinated by the spinal cord. During a reflex action, nerve impulses enter the spinal cord and are immediately directed back out of the spinal cord down a motor neuron. This 'short circuit' allows the body to respond to fear, pain or danger by making muscles move quickly.

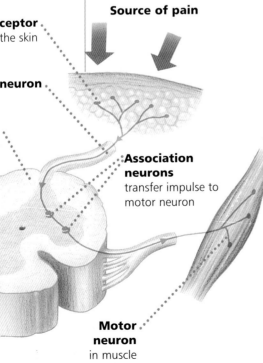

The brain is the body's
control centre

The brain is the control centre of the body and the place where thoughts take place and memories are stored. It is very soft and sits securely inside the skull. The brain is covered in tough protective membranes and also bathed in fluid, which supports it and protects it from damage. The brain is divided into three main areas: the brainstem, cerebellum and forebrain.

Cerebrum
is part of the forebrain
(see opposite page)

Corpus callosum
the bridge that connects
two halves of the cerebrum

Thalamus
is part of the
forebrain that sends
nerve impulses to the
cerebral cortex (see
page 14)

Hypothalamus
is part of the
forebrain

Brainstem
transfers nerve impulses
between the brain and
spinal cord

Cerebellum
controls
movement
and balance

Spinal cord
(see pages 10–11)

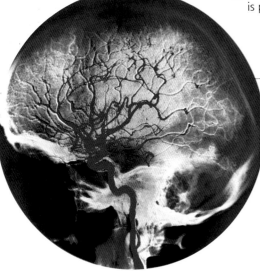

Brain blood vessels

The brain needs a lot of oxygen and nutrients to keep it functioning properly. Shown here in red are the blood vessels that supply the brain.

Brain areas

This cutaway shows the three main areas: the brainstem, cerebellum and the forebrain.

Special supply

The walls of the blood vessels that supply the brain form a barrier between the blood and the brain. This is so that no poisonous or foreign substances can get into the brain and damage it.

The forebrain

The forebrain has four distinct parts: the cerebrum (see opposite page), thalamus, hypothalamus and the limbic system. The thalamus recognises and sorts information that arrives in the brain and relays it to areas of the cerebrum. The hypothalamus (see pages 19 and 27) helps regulate many of the body's 'involuntary' functions, such as the control of body temperature. The limbic system (see pages 22–23) controls instincts and emotions.

Cerebrum cutaway

This view from the front of the cerebrum clearly shows the layers of grey and white matter.

White matter
is mainly made up of nerve fibres that link the cerebral cortex to the rest of the brain

Grey matter (cerebral cortex)
is rich in nerve cells

The largest part of the brain

The cerebrum is the largest part of the brain. It is where information is processed, where thought takes place, where memories are stored and decisions are made. The left and right side of the cerebrum are linked by a 'bridge' called the corpus callosum. Each side has a slightly different role (see below). The outer part of the cerebrum is called 'grey matter' (the cerebral cortex) and the inner layer is called 'white matter'.

The cerebellum

The cerebellum is part of the brain that works with the cerebrum to regulate smooth body movements. It also helps to make sure that we stay balanced. Without the cerebellum we would not be able to properly control the body.

LEFT AND RIGHT

The left and right sides of the brain control the opposite sides of the body. The two sides also have a number of specific functions. Musical and other artistic, creative and imaginative skills are mainly the responsibility of the right, while mathematical and speech skills are mainly the responsibility of the left. In most people fine control of the hand is also controlled by the left, which is why most people are right-handed.

Control crossover

The left or right side of the brain receives sensory information from the opposite side of the body and also sends instructions to muscles on the opposite side of the body.

Two halves

The two halves of the cerebrum, shown here, are often called hemispheres.

The brain receives and **processes information**

The brain is continually bombarded with nerve impulses from sense organs, such as the eyes, ears and skin. Information also comes from receptors inside the body. All this information is carried to the brain via the nerves of the peripheral nervous system and the spinal cord.

The cerebral cortex

Information is directed to different areas of the brain via the thalamus. For example, most of the sensory information the brain receives is processed by the surface layer of the cerebrum – the cerebral cortex. Areas in the middle and side of the cerebral cortex receive information about touch, taste, hearing and smell. Information from the eyes goes to an area at the back of the cerebrum called the visual cortex.

Parietal lobe
receives impulses from touch and pain receptors

Occipital lobe (visual cortex)
receives and analyses impulses from the eyes

Frontal lobe
controls speech and thought (see page 21)

Temporal lobe
receives and analyses impulses from the ears

Areas of the brain (external)
The surface of the brain – the cerebral cortex – is divided into four main lobes.

Judo practice
These judo students use the information sent to their brains from different sense organs to help overcome their opponents.

14

Understanding nerve impulses

To understand what is happening, the brain decodes nerve impulses, analyses them and compares them with stored memories. This information becomes the 'sensations' we experience. For example, we use information from the nose in order to understand our surroundings and to protect the body – if food has a bad smell we might decide not to eat it.

Brain response

Once the brain has analysed and understood the information, it makes decisions based on that information. It also stores the information it has received as memories (see pages 24–25) and sends instructions out to the body to respond.

Olfactory bulb
All the smell receptor nerve fibres meet in the olfactory bulb, which is an 'extension' of the brain (see page 22)

Nerve fibres
carry information about smell to the brain

Smell receptors
detect odour molecules in breathed-in air

Nostrils
are the entrance to the nose

Inside the nose

Smell receptors detect odour molecules and then send nerve impulses to the brain via the olfactory bulb. The brain analyses the impulses in a split second.

MAPPING THE BRAIN

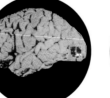

The modern, scientific approach to understanding the brain started in the late 19th century, when a French scientist called Pierre Broca investigated the brains of people who had speech problems. He found that a certain area of their brains had been damaged by disease. Other scientists looked at what happened when they cut into the brains of some patients or stimulated the brains of animals with electricity. In this way, the function of different parts of the brain began to be uncovered.

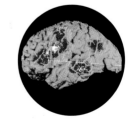

Brain scans

Since early 'brain maps' (see left), technology has developed so that we can take special images of brain activity.

Movement is co-ordinated by **the brain**

One of the most important things that the central nervous system does is to control movement. Every time we reach for something, walk or say a word, the central nervous system controls and co-ordinates the action of the body muscles to make the movement happen.

Motor control

The motor area of the cerebrum controls most complex movements. It lies in the middle and to the side of the cerebral cortex (see page 21). Different areas of this part of the brain control the movement of different parts of the body. Parts of the body that perform precise movements have more of this space devoted to them.

PARALYSIS

Paralysis happens when a person cannot move some or all of their muscles. It can occur if the brain is damaged by injury or if its blood supply is cut off temporarily. It also happens if the spinal cord is damaged and nerve impulses cannot travel between the brain and muscles. Diseases, such as polio, can also affect the nervous system and cause paralysis. Once the spinal cord or the brain is damaged the cells cannot usually be repaired.

Paraolympian

Paralysis does not mean that the brain stops working. This athlete is taking part in the Paraolympic Games, which are held every four years.

Learning to move

Many movements are complicated, involving the use of many muscles. Key movements, such as walking, are learnt in childhood. 'Programs' for different types of movement are stored in the brain, particularly in the cerebellum (see page 12). These programs are relayed to the cerebral cortex when we decide to move.

Skipping

Skipping may seem simple, but it involves highly co-ordinated, precisely timed movements of the body.

Keep practising

Movements, such as those used for ten-pin bowling, have to be learnt. If they are practised, the brain memorises what has to be done and gets better at repeating it.

Cerebellum

The cerebellum is vital in controlling movement and ensuring that our movements are smooth and accurate. It also helps control our posture and keeps us balanced.

Co-ordinating movements

To co-ordinate muscle movement the brain continually monitors the information it receives from sensors all over the body. The main sensors are inside the ear (which send nerve impulses about body position and balance) and inside muscles and tendons (which send nerve impulses about muscle movement and position). This information goes to the cerebellum, where it is processed and then sent to the motor areas of the cerebrum. The brain then sends out new instructions that 'fine tune' the body's movement.

The nervous system controls **body functions**

The nervous system controls many body functions without us being aware of it. For example, it co-ordinates the muscles of the digestive system as they move food along inside the body. The part of the nervous system that controls these 'involuntary' functions is called the autonomic nervous system.

Food ball
is made up of chewed and crushed food

Peristalsis

Muscles of the digestive system relax and contract forming a wave-like action called peristalsis. It is one function controlled by the autonomic nervous system.

Stomach
churns chewed food into a runny mixture

Small intestine
absorbs nutrients from food

Muscle wall
contracts and relaxes, slowly moving the food ball towards the stomach

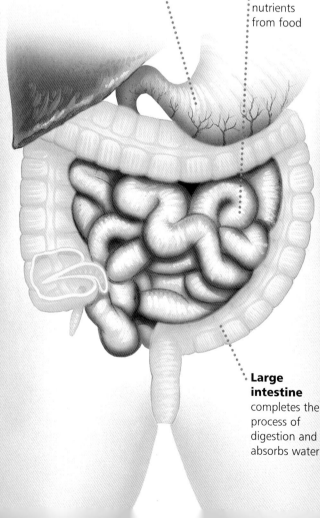

Autonomic nervous system

The autonomic nervous system helps control everything from heart rate and breathing to digestion and body temperature (see opposite page). It helps regulate how the organs in the body perform and helps to make sure everything inside the body works properly. The autonomic nervous system helps co-ordinate the activity of many parts of the body. For example, when we run, the autonomic nervous system automatically speeds up the heart rate, increases blood pressure and slows digestion down: all things that let us run faster.

Large intestine
completes the process of digestion and absorbs water

Digestion control

Different parts of the digestive system break down food and extract nutrients without us having to think about it. The autonomic nervous system helps to co-ordinate these processes.

Hypothalamus
regulates the autonomic
nervous system and the
endocrine system

Operational control

To control the
autonomic nervous
system the brain and
spinal cord process
information from the body.
Then they send instructions
along the nerves of the
autonomic nervous system.
The hypothalamus is the main area
of the brain that regulates this
process and also controls different
functions of the endocrine system
(see pages 26–27).

Cerebellum
helps to control
movement,
balance and
co-ordination

Brain stem
helps to control
breathing, heart
rate and blood
pressure

KEEPING COOL

Temperature control is one of the main jobs of
the hypothalamus, which contains special
receptors that monitor the body's temperature.
One of the most important jobs the autonomic
nervous system does is to help keep the body's
temperature at a constant 37 degrees Celsius.
For example, if you start to heat up, the
autonomic nervous system makes you sweat,
which cools the skin down. It also makes more
blood flow near the surface of your skin
(allowing the blood to cool down).

Working out

*The body can only work properly within a
small range of temperatures – if you get too
hot or too cold, you become ill. That is why
you sweat to keep cool when you exercise.*

We remember things, make decisions and
have opinions

The human brain can think, remember things, make decisions and have opinions, put ideas into words and plan for the future. The ability to have conscious thoughts like these means that humans are very good at dealing with complicated situations and ideas. It also gives us the ability to read and write, create inventions and produce works of art. Thinking also means that we are aware that we are individuals, each with our own unique personality.

Investigating the brain

Modern machines, such as this scanner, allow doctors to look at the brain and see if anything is wrong. But we still do not know exactly how it allows us to 'think'.

How do we think?

Scientists are still not entirely sure how the brain 'thinks' or exactly what parts are involved in this complicated process. However, it is clear that the areas of the brain where connections are made between new nerve impulses and stored memories play an important part. The part of the brain that controls speech is also very important (see opposite page).

Deep in thought

The brains of these chess players are working out how to win the game. To make decisions about their next moves, they are using their knowledge about the rules of chess, which they have had to learn.

Premotor cortex
controls precise movements,
such as using a games console

Motor cortex
controls muscle
movements

Frontal lobe
controls movements,
speech and thought

Broca's centre
is the speech
centre of the brain

Prefrontal cortex
plays a part in thought,
decision-making
and planning

Cerebellum
(see page 13)

Frontal lobes

The frontal lobes (located at the front of the cerebral cortex) are one of the most important parts of the brain. They are involved in thinking, planning and the control of certain types of behaviour. The frontal lobes receive nerve impulses from the rest of the brain and are closely linked to the limbic system, which is the centre of our emotions (see pages 22–23). It is also thought that one part of this lobe (the prefrontal cortex) plays a very important part in determining what kind of person we are – our personalities.

Frontal lobe (left side)

The frontal lobe is divided into four separate areas: the prefrontal cortex, the premotor cortex, the motor cortex and Broca's centre.

SPEECH

Words and language are a very important part of thinking. You can form words 'inside your head' and therefore shape your thoughts. The ability to speak is partly controlled by an area of the brain, called Broca's centre, which is located towards the front and on the side of the cerebral cortex. This part of the brain is linked to the motor area of the cerebral cortex that controls the muscles in the mouth, throat and chest that enable you to talk.

Learning to talk

This baby watches its mother's mouth as part of the process of learning to talk. When we want to tell people what we are thinking we turn our thoughts into speech.

The limbic system helps
produce emotions

Fear, pleasure, sadness and anger are just some of the feelings that we can experience. These emotions are very important because they help us to survive and make life exciting. It is thought that they are produced mainly by certain areas of the brain that form a ring, or network, inside the cerebrum. This network is called the limbic system.

Thalamus
sends nerve impulses to the cerebral cortex (see page 12)

Hypothalamus
helps control the autonomic nervous system and the endocrine system

Cerebrum
processes information (see page 13)

Olfactory bulb
links the sense of smell to memory

Hippocampus
helps to create memories (see page 25)

Amygdala
is thought to produce emotional 'feelings'

The limbic system

The limbic system not only controls emotions, but also triggers impulses to do things.

The limbic system

The limbic system is made up of structures, such as the amygdala and the hippocampus, linked with the hypothalamus. Little is known about how the limbic system works. However, it is clear that the structures are connected and work with other parts of the brain, such as the 'thinking' areas in the frontal lobe and the parts that are linked to memory, to give our thoughts their emotional content.

Basic emotion

Fear is one of the most basic emotions we feel and is very important because it helps us protect ourselves from danger. The way in which we feel fear gives an idea of how the limbic system works.

It is thought that the area of the brain that produces the feeling of fear is the amygdala. The amygdala receives sensory information – for example the sight of a scary place, such as a dark room – and recognises that it could mean 'danger'. It then sends nerve impulses that, for example, make the stomach 'lurch' with fear and help prepare the body to react.

Fear of open spaces

Some people are very frightened of certain things – such as open spaces or spiders. These 'phobias' are often caused by bad experiences in childhood.

THAT SMELL REMINDS ME OF...

Have you ever sensed a smell and almost immediately remembered something that happened to you, or felt a very strong emotion? For example, does the smell of sun cream remind you of a holiday? This type of experience occurs because the nerves that carry information about smell from the nose run close to the areas of the limbic system, which are linked with the creation of emotions and memory. Certain smells therefore trigger certain memories and emotions.

Smell familiar?

Strong smells, like that of the hot, sandy beach shown here, can trigger memories. Whether they are memories of good or bad times depends on the individual.

We have different types of
memory

All the knowledge and skills we possess have to be learned and then stored as memories. This store of information is vital for the thinking process. Learning happens from infancy as we try things out and acquire new skills. It is thought that learning happens when new connections are made between neurons in the brain.

Sensory memory

There are a number of different types of memory. Most of the information the brain gets from the senses is only held in the 'sensory memory' for less than a second – enough time for us to know where we are, so that we can move safely.

Short-term memory

Short-term memory lets us remember things – such as the name of something we have to look up in a book – for a few seconds. This kind of memory is used when we put thoughts into words.

Sensory memory

The day-to-day sensory information the brain receives is only briefly stored in the memory.

Memory transfer

As this child plays, he stores information in his short-term memory. However, if certain actions are repeated, the skills may be transferred to his long-term memory.

Long-term memory

We store information in the long-term memory by repeating it often. We can keep this information for years, although remembering it can take some time. However, information that is used often from the long-term memory can be remembered quickly. Nobody knows exactly where all the facts and skills we can remember are stored. However, it is thought that the cerebral cortex and the cerebellum are involved, and that the hippocampus (in the limbic system, see page 22) helps.

Playing an instrument

When learning a new skill, such as playing a musical instrument, practising helps us to store it in the long-term memory.

SLEEP AND DREAMS

When you go to sleep, your brain does not stop working. It is not known exactly what the brain does while you sleep, but without it your brain would have problems thinking and doing things. Scientists believe that sleep is the time when the brain processes the day's events and sorts and stores information. This may be the reason people dream. Brain activity changes through the night (see below) as you move through stages of light sleep (coloured light blue) and deep sleep (coloured dark blue).

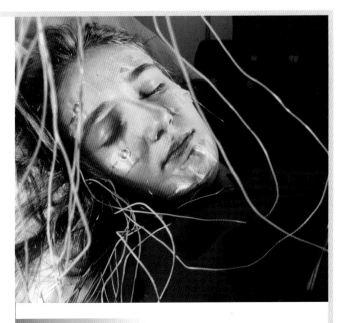

Brain activity

Special machines that are attached to a patient can be used to monitor brain activity during sleep (see below).

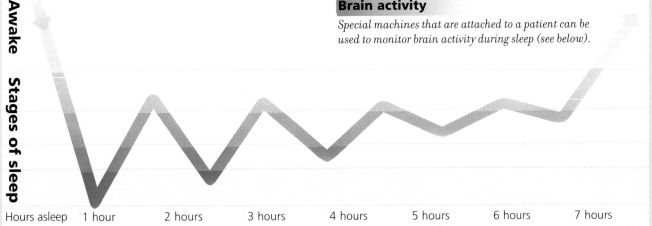

Awake							
Stages of sleep							
Hours asleep	1 hour	2 hours	3 hours	4 hours	5 hours	6 hours	7 hours

The brain is linked to the
endocrine system

The brain controls many of the things that happen in the body through the nervous system. However, the brain is also linked to another system that influences what goes on in the body. This is called the endocrine system.

Chemical messengers

The nervous system uses nerve impulses sent via nerves to carry instructions and information around the body. The endocrine system uses chemicals called hormones. These 'chemical messengers' are mainly produced by endocrine glands (see page 28). They are carried in the blood to the specific part of the body they affect.

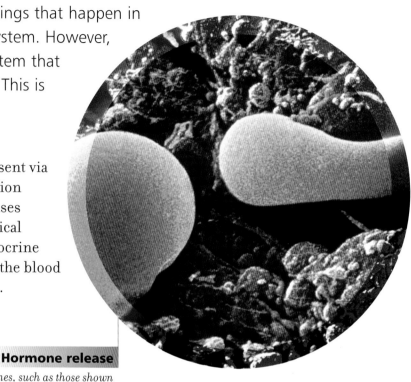

Hormone release

Hormones, such as those shown here (yellow) are released directly into the bloodstream by endocrine glands.

Important functions

The endocrine system controls many different functions in the body, from how the body uses the nutrients in the food we eat, to the production of the sperm and eggs that allows adults to have babies. One of the most important roles of the endocrine system is keeping the chemicals in the body at the right level. For example, the hormones insulin and glucagon are produced by the pancreas and help balance the amount of sugar in the blood at the right level (see page 29).

Nutrient management

When we eat food, hormones in the body adjust chemical levels in the blood so they remain balanced.

Hormone release

The brain is linked to the endocrine system, primarily through the hypothalamus. The hypothalamus produces hormones itself and also controls the pituitary gland (to which it is attached). The pituitary gland releases a variety of hormones, some of which control body functions directly. Others control the function of other endocrine glands. For this reason, the pituitary gland is often called the 'chief' endocrine gland.

Because the brain and endocrine system are linked, hormones can have an effect on our moods and behaviour, while mental processes (such as fear) can affect the production of hormones (see below).

Nerve fibres
link the hypothalamus to the pituitary gland

Posterior lobe
stores and releases hormones

Anterior lobe
produces hormones

Blood vessels
transport hormones to the rest of the body in the bloodstream

Pituitary gland (cutaway)

The pituitary gland has two lobes, the anterior (which produces hormones) and the posterior (which stores and releases hormones produced by the hypothalamus).

FIGHT OR FLIGHT

When your brain experiences feelings, such as fear or stress, it sends nerve impulses to the adrenal glands, which produce the hormone adrenaline. Unlike most other hormones, adrenaline is fast acting and produces a number of effects: it increases heart rate, makes more blood flow to the limbs and increases the amount of sugar in the blood. All these things prepare the body to fight or run away.

Face off

Adrenaline levels rise as a result of stress, for example, when we cannot find what we want while out shopping. This can lead to heated arguments!

Endocrine glands produce
hormones

Hormones – the body's chemical messengers – are produced in endocrine glands, which release them directly into the blood. The main endocrine glands are the hypothalamus (see pages 19 and 27), the pituitary (see page 27), the thyroid (which produces the hormone that helps control how the body uses energy it gets from food), the pair of adrenal glands (see page 27), the pancreas (see below) and the reproductive glands – the ovaries and testes (which produce hormones that control sexual functions).

Carrying messages

Some hormones are released at specific times, for example, at the start of puberty. They trigger the production of sperm and eggs.

Cell receptor site

Target cell

Hormone
in the blood

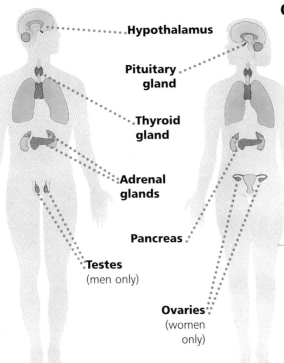

Hypothalamus

Pituitary gland

Thyroid gland

Adrenal glands

Pancreas

Testes
(men only)

Ovaries
(women only)

On target

Hormones travel around the body in the blood and, although they reach all the different parts of the body, each hormone only makes things happen in specific tissues. For example, insulin, produced by the pancreas, makes the liver store glucose (a type of sugar that the body gets from food).

Endocrine glands

Endocrine glands are sited all over the body, producing different hormones at different times. These are just some of the glands.

Target lock on

A hormone only affects its 'target' tissues. The cells of these tissues have shaped 'receptor sites' into which only the hormone's molecules can fit: like a key in a lock.

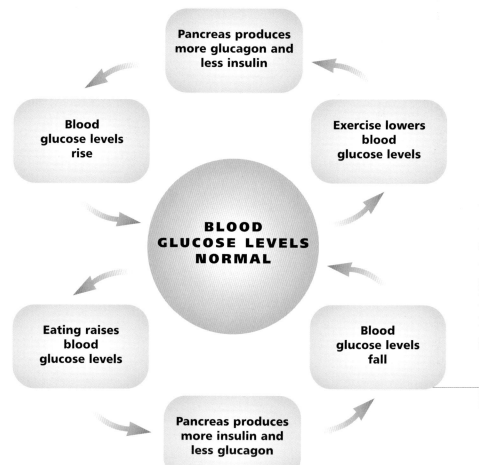

Pancreas produces more glucagon and less insulin

Blood glucose levels rise

Exercise lowers blood glucose levels

BLOOD GLUCOSE LEVELS NORMAL

Eating raises blood glucose levels

Blood glucose levels fall

Pancreas produces more insulin and less glucagon

The feedback loop

The action of hormones is often controlled by a 'feedback loop'. For example, the rise or fall of glucose levels in the blood is sensed by cells in the pancreas. The pancreas then produces more or less hormones (insulin and glucagon) to bring levels of glucose back to normal. Insulin makes the liver store glucose, while glucagon raises levels of blood glucose because it makes the liver release glucose into the blood.

Glucose balance

This is just one example of a feedback loop. Each loop ensures that hormones are produced when required and that the levels of hormones remain balanced.

DIABETES

If the glands of the endocrine system malfunction then many things can go wrong. Diabetes is one example of a problem that occurs when the body does not produce a hormone – in this case insulin – properly or if the body's cells do not respond normally to it. In diabetes, blood glucose levels become too high and the person feels thirsty and hungry, and can lose weight and become tired.

Treating the effects

Diabetes can occur in young people and adults. Its effects can be treated by a regular insulin injection, shown here, and dietary changes.

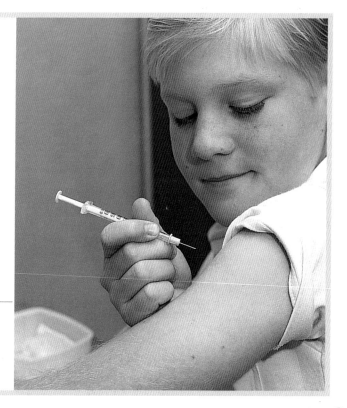

Glossary

Adrenal glands A pair of endocrine glands located on the top of the kidneys. They produce hormones, including adrenaline.

Amygdala A small almond-shaped structure in the limbic system, thought to produce feelings of fear.

Association neuron A type of neuron that relays impulses from one neuron to another.

Autonomic nervous system The part of the nervous system that automatically controls body functions, such as the heart rate.

Brain The control centre of the nervous system, made up of billions of nerve cells.

Brainstem The region where the brain and spinal cord meet. It helps control vital body functions such as heart beat and breathing.

Central nervous system The part of the nervous system made up of the brain and the spinal cord. It co-ordinates and controls the body.

Cerebellum The part of the brain that controls balance and movement.

Cerebral cortex The surface layer of the cerebrum.

Cerebrum The largest part of the brain that co-ordinates things, such as thoughts and actions.

Dendrite The part of a neuron that carries nerve impulses towards its cell body.

Electroencephalograph (EEG) A machine that measures electrical activity produced by the brain.

Endocrine gland A structure inside the body that produces and secretes hormones directly into the blood.

Endocrine system The system of glands and organs that secrete hormones. It controls many of the basic functions of the body.

Glucagon A hormone secreted by cells in the pancreas that causes the liver to release stored glucose into the blood.

Glucose A type of sugar that the body gets from food.

Grey matter Areas of the central nervous system made up of the cell bodies of neurones, for example, the cerebral cortex.

Hormones Chemicals produced by endocrine glands that alter the activity of various organs in the body. Hormones are 'chemical messengers' that are carried by the blood.

Hippocampus A structure in the brain that is involved with the regulation of emotions and the formation of long-term memory.

Hypothalamus A part of the brain that monitors and regulates many basic body functions, such as temperature and water balance.

Insulin A hormone secreted by cells in the pancreas that causes the body to store glucose.

Limbic system A group of brain structures that work to help regulate emotion and memory.

Motor neuron A type of neuron that carries nerve impulses from the brain and spinal cord to muscles or organs.

Nerve A bundle of nerve fibres.

Nerve impulse An electrical signal that travels along a neuron. Nerve impulses carry information and instructions around the nervous system.

Neuron A nerve cell. Billions of neurons make up the nervous system. They carry nerve impulses.

Pancreas A gland that is part of the digestive system. It contains cells that produce the hormones insulin and glucagon.

Peripheral nervous system The part of the nervous system made up of nerves that connects the brain and spinal cord to the rest of the body.

Pituitary gland An important endocrine gland that produces a number of hormones, some of which control body functions.

Sensory neuron A type of neuron that carries nerve impulses to the brain and spinal cord from sensory receptors in the sense organs and other parts of the body.

Soft tissue 'Soft' areas of the body not made up of bone and cartilage, such as the brain.

Spinal cord The tube of nerve tissue that runs down the back of the body from the base of the brain to the lower back. It is the main communication route between the brain and the rest of the body.

Synapse a junction between two neurons or between a neuron and muscle fibre. The synapse contains a small gap across which chemicals can flow to 'pass on' nerve impulses.

Thyroid gland An endocrine gland found in the neck that produces hormones that, for example, stimulate growth.

White matter Areas of the central nervous system made up of nerve fibres.

Find out more

These are just some of the websites where you can find out more information about the heart. Many of the websites also provide information and illustrations about other systems and processes of the human body.

Note to parents and teachers
Every effort has been made by the Publishers to ensure that these websites are suitable for children; that they are of the highest educational value, and that they contain no inappropriate or offensive material. However, because of the nature of the Internet, it is impossible to guarantee that the contents of these sites will not be altered. We strongly advise that Internet access is supervised by a responsible adult.

www.medtropolis.com
This Virtual Body website includes an animation of the heart in action that can be speeded up or slowed down, as would happen during or after exercise.

www.hyperstaffs.info/ science/work/durber
Use this website to see an animation of how the blood transports oxygen, carbon dioxide and glucose, and interact to keep 'Ernie' alive.

www.smm.org/heart
Interact with this Habits of the Heart website to, for example, find the heartbeat with a virtual stethoscope.

www.brainpop.com/ health/circulatorysystem
Movies, quizzes and lots more information about the circulatory system, blood pressure, blood donations, and more.

www.bbc.co.uk/ education/medicine/
This 'Medicine Through Time' website includes Dr William Harvey's discovery of blood circulation and much more about anatomy and surgery during the 17th century.

http://vilenski.org/ science/humanbody
Join in the Human Body Adventure to discover more about the blood, heart and how other parts of the body work.

www.planet-science.com/ outthere/index.html?page =/outthere/bodybeat/ fitness_factory/heart.html
This website investigates the heart, fitness and exercise.

http://fi.edu/biosci/blood/
This Franklin Institute website provides highly detailed information about the heart and circulatory system.

www.amnh.org/ nationalcenter/infection
An interactive website all about microbes, including those germs that can invade the body and cause diseases if not stopped by the body's defence systems.

http://www.blood.co.uk/ pages/e13basic.html
Find out all about blood on this website from The National Blood Service. It includes an explanation of the different blood groups, blood transfusions, and a section about how blood donations are used.

http://kidshealth.org/ teen/your_body/ body_basics/spleen.html
How the spleen and lymphatic system works are just some of the body parts explained here, along with links to the circulatory system.

Index

adrenal glands 27, 28
amygdala 22, 23
association neurons 10, 11
autonomic nervous system 18–19
  motor neurons 6
axons 8

backbone 10
blood 26, 27, 28, 29
blood vessels 9, 12
body temperature 12, 18, 19
brain 10, 14, 19, 24, 31
  analyses nerve impulses 9, 15
  areas 4, 12, 14, 16, 21, 22, 31
  control of body functions 4, 6, 7, 18, 21, 26
  control of movement 4, 6, 7, 14, 16–17
  electrical signals *see entry for* brain waves
  grey matter 13
  health 5, 31
  lobes 14, 21, 22
  mapping 15, 31
  memories 6, 7, 12, 13, 15, 20, 22
  protection 4, 12
  response 15
  sides 13
  thoughts 12, 13, 20, 21, 24
  white matter 13
brain damage 15
brain scan 4, 15, 20
brainstem 12, 19
brain waves 5, 25
Broca, Pierre 15, 31
Broca's centre 21

central nervous system 6, 7, 8, 16
cerebellum 12, 13, 17, 19, 25
cerebral cortex 12, 13, 14, 16, 17, 21, 22, 25
cerebrum 4, 12, 13, 14, 16, 17, 22
chemical messengers *see entry for* hormones
corpus callosum 12, 13

dendrites 8, 9

diabetes 29
digestion 5, 12, 18
dreams 25

electroencephalograph 5
emotions and feelings 4, 5, 11, 12, 21, 22–23, 27
endocrine glands 26, 27, 28–29
endocrine system 5, 19, 26–27, 29

feelings and emotions 4, 5, 11, 12, 21, 22–23, 27
forebrain 12
  cerebrum 4, 12, 13, 14, 16, 17, 22
  hypothalamus 12, 19, 22, 27, 28
  limbic system 12, 21, 22–23, 25
  thalamus 12, 14
frontal lobe 14, 21, 22

hippocampus 22, 25
hormones 5, 26, 27, 28, 29
  adrenaline 27
  glucagon 26, 29
  insulin 26, 28, 29
hypothalamus 12, 19, 22, 27, 28

involuntary functions 6, 18

limbic system 12, 21, 22–23

memories 6, 7, 12, 13, 15, 20, 22
memory 24–25
  long-term 25
  sensory 24
  short-term 24
motor cortex 21
motor neurons 6, 7, 8, 9, 11
muscle fibre 8, 9
muscles 6, 7, 8, 11, 13, 16, 17, 18, 21

nerve cells *see entry for* neurons
nerve fibres 11, 13, 15; *also see entry for* neurons, axons
nerve impulses 5, 7, 9, 11, 12, 15, 16, 19, 20, 22, 26

received by the brain 6, 10, 14, 17
  sent from the brain 6, 10
nerves 4, 5, 6, 7, 8–9, 10, 26
nervous system 6–7, 16, 18, 26
neurons (nerve cells) 4, 5, 6, 8, 9, 24
  axons 8
  cell body 8
  dendrites 8, 9

occipital lobe (visual cortex) 14
olfactory bulb 15, 22

pancreas 26, 28, 29
paralysis 16
parietal lobe 14
peripheral nervous system 6, 7, 8, 14
personality 20, 21
pituitary gland 27, 28
prefrontal cortex 21
premotor cortex 21

reflex action 11
reproductive glands 28

sense organs 14
sensory memory 24
sensory neurons 6, 8, 9, 11
sensory receptor 9, 11, 14
skin 8
skull 4, 10, 12
sleep 25
speech 15, 21
spinal cord 4, 6, 7, 8, 9, 10–11, 12, 14, 19
  damage 16
spinal nerves 6, 10, 11
synapses 9

temporal lobe 14
thalamus 12, 14, 22
thyroid 28

vertebrae 10, 11
visual cortex *see entry for* occipital lobe